I0795550

XTREME SPORTS

BMX

BY BRYAN LANGDO

EPIC

EPIC, AN IMPRINT OF BELLWETHER MEDIA BY FLUTTERBEE

EPIC

EPIC BOOKS are no ordinary books. They burst with intense action, high-speed heroics, and shadows of the unknown. Are you ready for an Epic adventure?

This edition first published in 2027 by Bellwether Media, Inc.

Text copyright © 2027 by Bellwether Media, Inc. All rights reserved. No part of this publication may be reproduced, stored in any retrieval system, or transmitted in any form or by any means, electronic, mechanical, photocopying, recording, or otherwise, without written permission of the publisher.

EPIC and associated logos are trademarks and/or registered trademarks of Bellwether Media, Inc. Bellwether Media is a division of FlutterBee Education Group.

For information regarding permission, write to Bellwether Media, Inc., Attention: Permissions Department, 3500 American Blvd W, Suite 150, Bloomington, MN 55431.

Library of Congress Cataloging-in-Publication Data is available at www.loc.gov or upon request from the publisher.

ISBN: 9798898800963 (hardcover)
ISBN: 9798898802202 (ebook)

Editor: Kieran Downs Designer: Jeffrey Kollock

Printed in the United States of America, North Mankato, MN.

TABLE OF CONTENTS

RACE TIME!

A crowd cheers as riders race around a dirt track. Their bikes are small but fast.

The riders zip around turns. They launch off jumps and fly through the air. This is BMX!

ALL IN THE NAME

The name BMX stands for "bicycle motocross."

WHAT IS BMX?

The two main kinds of BMX **competition** are racing and **freestyle**.

Races take place on dirt tracks. Freestyle riders perform tricks on bikes. These events happen in freestyle bike parks.

FAMOUS LOCATION

CHULA VISTA BMX TRACK

LOCATION	Chula Vista, California, United States
FAMOUS FOR	BMX track that hosts local and national events

BMX bikes are smaller than most other bikes. The seats are low. Riders almost never sit on them.

BMX GEAR

Riders wear pads on their elbows, knees, and shins. They also wear helmets.

THE HISTORY OF BMX

SCHWINN KRATES

In 1968, the Schwinn bike company released the Sting-Ray Krate. Kids raced these bikes on dirt tracks.

In 1969, a BMX race was held in Los Angeles, California. This was the first organized BMX race.

ON ANY SUNDAY

On Any Sunday is a 1971 movie about motorcycle racing. The opening shows kids riding bikes on a dirt track. It helped make BMX popular.

TIMELINE

1968 Schwinn releases the Sting-Ray Krate

1981 The International BMX Federation is formed

1995 Freestyle BMX is a part of the first X Games

2008 BMX racing is added to the Summer Olympics

2021 Freestyle BMX becomes an Olympic sport

By the 1970s, BMX was popular all over the United States. Some riders rode their bikes in skate parks. Freestyle BMX was born.

People formed **leagues**. In 1981, the **International BMX Federation** was formed.

skate park

2009 X GAMES

2025 X GAMES

In 1995, freestyle BMX was a part of the first **X Games**. Famous riders helped the sport grow.

WOMEN'S BMX RACING, 2008 SUMMER OLYMPICS

BMX racing was added to the **Summer Olympics** in 2008. In 2021, freestyle BMX became an Olympic sport.

BMX TODAY

Freestyle BMX riders take turns competing. Each rider has 60 seconds to perform tricks. They jump, slide, spin, and flip.

Judges give them points. The rider with the most points wins.

HOW TO

BUNNY HOP

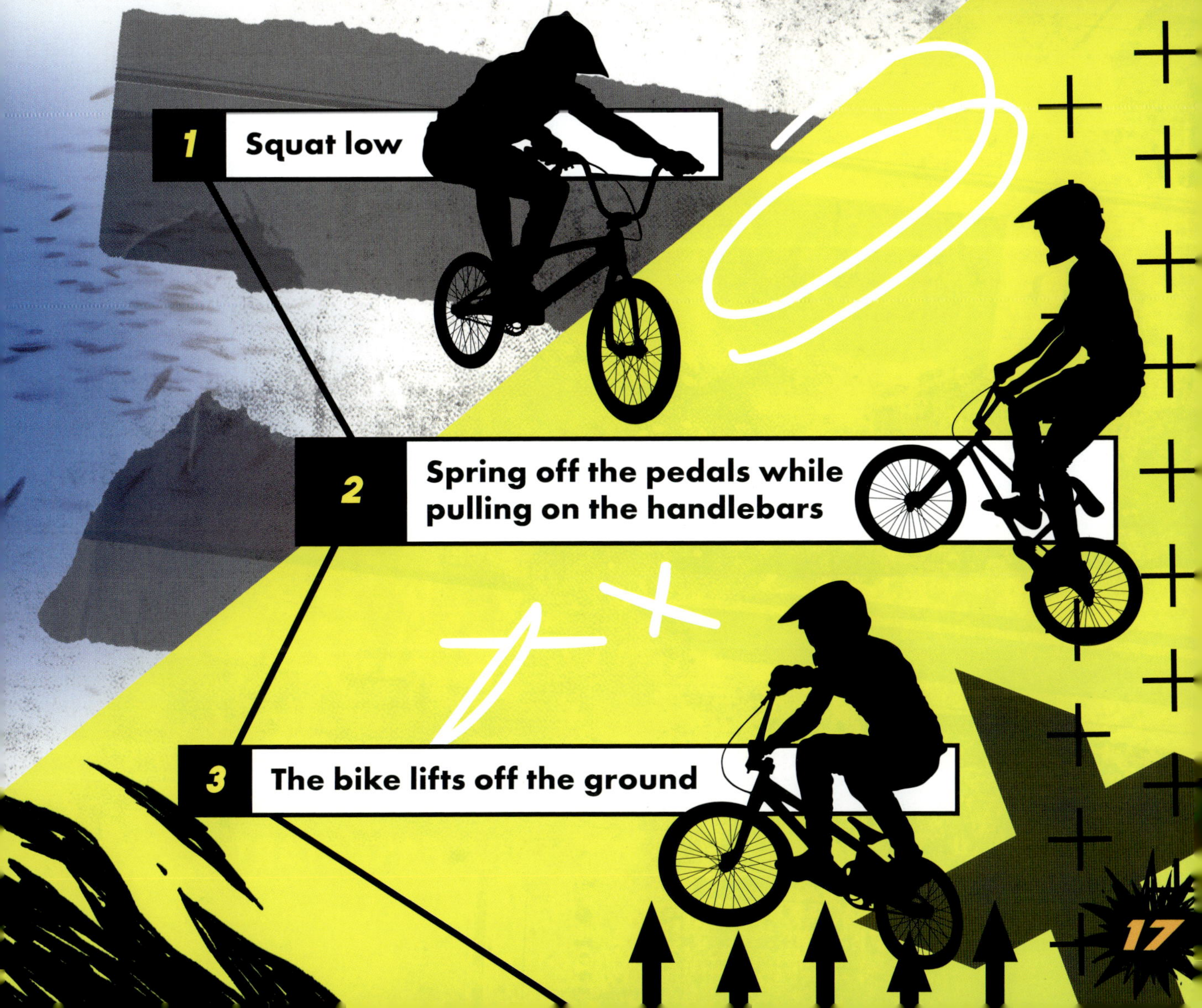

BMX racetracks have eight lanes. Riders start at a gate. The riders drop down the start ramp all at once.

The track has sharp turns and small hills. The first rider to cross the finish line wins.

A FAST START

The start ramps in BMX races are up to 26 feet (8 meters) tall.

FAMOUS FACE

MAT HOFFMAN

BIRTHDAY	January 9, 1972
HOMETOWN	Edmond, Oklahoma
FAMOUS FOR	Freestyle rider known for inventing many tricks and winning many competitions

2021 UCI BMX WORLD CHAMPIONSHIPS

The UCI BMX World **Championships** take place every year. There are races and freestyle competitions.

The world's best riders compete. These amazing riders are skilled, fast, and fearless!

GLOSSARY

championships—contests to decide the best team or person

competition—an event in which someone tries to win something someone else is trying to win

freestyle—related to events based on tricks rather than time

International BMX Federation—a former group that was in charge of BMX racing around the world

leagues—large groups of athletes or sports teams that often play one other

Summer Olympics—a worldwide summer sports contest held in a different country every four years

X Games—a yearly extreme sports contest featuring many different sports

TO LEARN MORE

AT THE LIBRARY

Amstutz, Lisa J. *The Gearhead's Guide to BMX Bikes.* North Mankato, Minn.: Capstone, 2023.

Vonder Brink, Tracy. *BMX.* Minneapolis, Minn.: Jump!, 2025.

Walker, Hubert. *BMX Racing.* Mendota Heights, Minn.: Apex, 2022.

ON THE WEB

FACTSURFER

Factsurfer.com gives you a safe, fun way to find more information.

1. Go to www.factsurfer.com.
2. Enter "BMX" into the search box and click .
3. Select your book cover to see a list of related content.

INDEX

The images in this book are reproduced through the courtesy of: homydesign, front cover, pp. 1, 4, 5, 8, 8 (googles), 9, 18 (inset); Vasyl, front cover, p. 1; Aerial Specialized, p. 2; snaptitude, p. 3; shulers, pp. 6, 18; Zamrznuti tonovi, p. 6 (inset); Sherry V Smith, p. 7 (all); Northern life, p. 8 (bike); Marko, p. 8 (helmet); M.studio, p. 9 (elbow pads, knee pads); Kadmy, p. 9 (shin pads); artistmac/ Flickr, p. 10; Dominick Corrado, p. 11; Movieposterdb/ Wikimedia Commons, p. 11 (FF); Nels Olsen/ Flickr, p. 12 (1968); Buzz Pictures/ Alamy Stock Photo, pp. 12 (1995), 19 (right); CARL DE SOUZA/ Getty Images, p. 12 (2008); PA Images/ Alamy Stock Photo, pp. 12 (2021), 15; J.A. Dunbar, p. 13; Christian Pondella/ Getty Images, p. 14 (inset); Icon Sportswire/ Getty Images, p. 14; Konrad Swierad, p. 16; roibu, p. 16 (inset); Larry Busacca/ Getty Images, p. 19 (left); Amanda Edwards/ Getty Images, p. 19 (bottom); BSR Agency/ Getty Images, pp. 20, 21 (all).